FIGMENTS

Poems By Gerald George

Copyright 2014 by Gerald George

All rights reserved. No part of this book may be reproduced without the express, written consent of the author.

Published by The Piscataqua Press
An imprint of Riverrun Bookstore, Inc.
142 Fleet Street | Portsmouth, NH | 03801

www.piscataquapress.com
www.riverrunbookstore.com

Printed in the United States of America

ISBN: 978-1-939739-52-0

Cover photos by Ray Beal

To Carol Maryan-George

ACKNOWLEDGEMENTS

I am greatly indebted to the poet Richard Miles for insight and advice, to poets Paddy Bushe and William Carpenter for encouragement and support, to the poetry group of Sunrise Senior College at the University of Maine at Machias for helpful criticism, and for all her support to my wife Carol.

I am also grateful to the editors of the following publications for permission to reprint poems that originally appeared, or will appear, in their periodicals:
> *The Café Review* ("After old Archibald," "He just kept buying")
> *Gargoyle Magazine* ("Where did the cat go?")
> *Hiram Poetry Review* ("At eighty-four")
> *Literary Juice* ("Edna's son gave her")
> *The Main Street Rag* ("Driving through")
> *Saranac Review* ("After his wife")
> *Verse Wisconsin* ("Seize the day").

PREFACE:

What Are Figments?

Webster's Third describes a "figment" as "something made up, fabricated, or contrived." That will do.

They began coming in the late summer or early fall of 2011. They continued coming, obsessively, through all of 2012 into February 2013. Some have said that deaths led to the *Figments*: a brother and my two closest friends of longstanding. That time stands unrelieved. But the deaths caused the *Figments* only by opening me more readily to questions they raise. What accounts for them are the way things are. They will not be "fixed" by "fixing" me.

These poems use no rhyme, rhythm, or conventional line breaks except in short, set-off segments. In these passages I take on attitudes that in the twenty-first century are no longer tenable. Otherwise the form of the *Figments* minimally arrests their flow, or promotes it. From this, I hope, they derive their force.

Gerald George
September 2014

CONTENTS

Part One
Up in the clouds	1
After old Archibald	2
Driving through	3
Edna's son gave her	4
Seize the day	5
He was crazy	6
He just kept buying	7
He cupped his hands	8
The breaking up	9
The little cup came	10

Part Two
That didn't shake him	13
All of a sudden	14
At eighty-four	15
No car crash	16
It began when one day	17
That morning	18
Sitting in the river	19
The teddy bear sat	20
He had reached	21
She wanted to listen	22

Part Three
Once he saw	25
The night became	26
He sat there	27
What sense did it make	28
As he was making	29
What he thought	30
How wonderful!	31
They shut him out	33
The damned cork	34
She sat and fidgeted	35

Part Four
If he stared	39
What a breeze	40
Immediately he recognized	41
They had always told him	42
At last	43

Be careful	44
At first	45
Just stay calm	46
He liked to sit	47
So when they told her	48

Part Five

Magnificently huge	51
After his wife	52
The older he got	53
It troubled him	54
Try games	55
As he sat	56
They said he was	57
They told him such	58
It amazed him how	59
Where did the cat go?	60

Part Six

Sports can be	63
They told him	64
Illusion	65
She kept putting	66
And the sun	67
Conversing he discovered	68
Meadowlarks and mourning	69
Freezing wind blew	70
The assembled bones	71
They're down in the cellar	72

Part Seven

In the yellow-bright flicker	75
He understood	76
He had merely	77
They wanted us	78
He hated when	79
He began	80
That evening	81
Thunder over	82
You must perfect	83
She heard them out	84

Part Eight
Absurd, they said   87
One child   88
And he remembered   89
And the snow   90
What was less   91
How he loved   92
The waters flowed   93
Or was he merely   94
Suddenly   95
Goodbye now   96

About the Author   97

PART ONE

Up in the clouds

Up in the clouds on that day when
the sun infused them with light, the
white birches shone all standing out in
the green dark forest of spruce, all
reaching, and he stopped and listened and
heard it, so cold-bright-clear as if the
wind were strumming an icicle
xylophone, the sound of song antiphonal
between sap and atmosphere, leaf and
lightning, root and storm, and he heard
all through the swift night the deer, this
deer, that deer, herds of bounding
deer in the moon-ignited mountains, this
mountain, that mountain, ranges of
mountains capped with shining snow, shouting
up to the zillion shining stars, and he bowed
down and tried to close his eyes because so
much shining was blinding, and he tried to
cover his ears because so loud the
sound became as if all the shining
everywhere vibrated all at once, and the
least weed, the weakest thistle, the lowliest
stalk all joined in a vastness of voices:
O hope for me!

After old Archibald

After old Archibald put in an espresso
machine, all the poets in town sat in Archibald's
Grocery and Gas drinking espresso and
reading each other's poems that pissed and
moaned because of the state of the
world and how damned man is by
his own nature when, one day, old
Missus Archibald forgot again which
was the gas and which was the brake and
drove her three thousand pounds of steel and
chrome through the plate-glass window at
Archibald's and maimed some of
the poets, and the others scrambled
around and wondered how they got to
be so lucky considering how
bad the world was, but soon they started
drinking espresso again and writing
poems that went on pissing and
moaning, and Missus Archibald, too,
they say, has taken to writing poems,
mostly about geraniums, hummingbirds, and
the shiny-bright light of heaven.

Driving through

Driving through countryside, past old
houses, many empty, and falling-down
barns and yards full of rusty junk, he
had the sudden sensation that people now
somehow walked beside his moving
car, farmers and their wives of earlier
times, scores of years, maybe
hundreds before, all in worn-out
clothes, moving beside him as if going with
him somewhere, and when he sped, they
sped, went faster as he went faster, until
he saw they would keep up no matter
what, that he could not get beyond
them, and yet none ever threatened or
even looked in his direction, but still he felt
fear as the throng kept growing, especially
through towns where streets grew choked with
people from other eras, and as he went
on, thousands who had lived before him ran
right beside him and then he knew that
when he got home and stopped, they, too,
would stop, would stay all about his
house, not bother him, but just stay, waiting,
until whatever eventually happened to him
happened.

Edna's son gave her

Edna's son gave her one, so before
long Morgan asked his son to get
him one, and soon, one after another, almost
everyone at the Eldercare Hotel got
one until the halls seemed filled with
wheelchairs coming and going, the
motorized ones whizzing, and of
course the staff tried to restrict wheelchairs to
those who needed them, but, who
did not need one?—why should
anyone hobble about on a walker when
one could race around in a
mechanized go-cart with three
speeds forward and a buzzer to
warn people out of the way just as
if the drivers were—look out!—fully
alive, but then Morgan and Edna had
a head-on crash, and so the caregivers said
no more wheelchairs, someone might get
hurt, we can't have that, so everyone had
to go back to crutches, couches, tapioca,
bingo, and reruns of
"This Is Your Life."

Seize the day

Seize the day, live in the moment, suck
all you can out of the dripping teat, that
was his answer to the inevitable, but
his eighties, nineties, the end didn't seem to
come, and the teat withered, and living
had less and less to do with seizing and
sucking, and at his 100th birthday party only
assisted-living techs showed up because
he'd outlived family and friends, and his
doctors were busy elsewhere helping other
people gain long life, and his health
prohibited cake and champagne, which
made him wonder a bit, especially after
he went blind and deaf and couldn't
watch TV ball games anymore, but at
one-hundred-and-five he could still play a
sort of shadowy croquet within his inner
cranium and take up the pleasure of thinking
that, just possibly, he might become the
oldest man still living in his home county or
country or—anywhere—maybe—
seize on that!

He was crazy

He was crazy, they all said so,
but—the apocalypse, the coming
Huns, unstoppable viruses, nuclear
war, a huge meteorite headed
right here, whatever, he went to
the woods to dig out a place for
his lead box, but the bones!—the
femurs, knuckles, skulls, all where he
wanted to bury the lead box full of
Shakespeare, Rembrandt, Bach, "the
best of man's expression"—and no
matter if no one ever found the box, no
survivor, no space visitor, because,
whatever happened, *"our best would
still exist"*;
and so he dug and that's when he
found them—the hundreds of
human skeletons, spent bullets in,
under, around the victims piled beneath
sod in a shallow ditch where the killers
thought the evidence would never
be found, but he had found them—
the bones!

He just kept buying

He just kept buying them in
antique stores, the old framed
photoed faces with no names on the
back, so many displaced identities, of
course he felt he had to buy them, but
why rescue them only to leave them in
oblivion, and so he kept buying and
putting them all over the walls of his
house, wondering, until one day it
came to him—even nameless, they
were,
with eyes, expressions, hats, mustaches,
uniforms, parasols—and he went out to
more shops and got more photos to put up on
more walls of staring people who no
longer had to be anything more than they
appeared.

He cupped his hands

He cupped his hands around
his eyes, out alone where he could
plainly see billowing fluffy clouds that
wandered the sky, changing from
shape to shape, whale to
wolf to giant sloth to head of a
something never before imagined that
turned over and looked at him, right
into his eyes, and said—"What do
you think you see?"—but that was not
always what it said, for sometimes the
indefinite white-dazzle shape with
blue-sky eyes and a wild red horizon of
a mouth asked him—"What do you think
you will ever see?"—which was not
always what it said either, for sometimes
it said, speaking as if it were all of the
unexpected shapes that clouds can
make—"We can tell you what you don't
see"—and that is when he knew from the
look on the face of this glowering shape that
whatever it saw that he didn't see, he
didn't want to see it.

The breaking up

The breaking up—yes, the unpredictables at
the core of quantum physics, the
irrational grip of the subconscious, the end of
representation in the visual arts, poetry so
chaotic that who knew any more what a
poem was, and also the world wars and the
Holocaust and nuclear bombs and now global
warming and terrorists and even down the
street he noticed a recent infestation of
feral neighbors and—well—he had to save his
mind from the continuous assault of everything
breaking up so he sat down and said:
    I will listen to nothing more
    about anything, period,
which seemed actually to work once he had
stopped his daily newspaper, cancelled his
other subscriptions, thrown out his books,
unplugged his radio and TV, rigged his phone to
give a continuously busy signal, opened no
mail that didn't have checks inside, spoke to
no one, and turned off all his lights, and then, as
he waited, he felt incredibly content. Yes.
As he waited.

The little cup came

The little cup came around again and
as she looked within it she noticed—she
really noticed—the shapes, some
round, some oblong, some hexagonal, and
the colors, mostly white but a couple of
shades of orange and one bright red, as
if to stand out, to shout—"Take first this
little gem!"—but why take any, why not
just look at the perfection of their
shapes, the pleasance of their colors, the
extraordinary fact of their sheer
existence, in a cup, for her, and suddenly
she shook from the thrill of it all, as if
they appeared for the first time to her
now-open eyes, and she called out (as
best she could)—"See? I see such
remarkable, remarkable . . ."—and
then she heard herself say to
herself—"such strangeness"—because
it all seemed strange, her old hand, her
sleeping gown, the wheelchair, the
slender bed, the glass of water, and
the again-insistent voice that she
heard urging her to swallow the
strange little colored shapes in
the strange cup.

PART TWO

That didn't shake him

That didn't shake him, the sight of
the dead fawn, haunches eaten by some
coyote, because he had earlier seen
    the full beauty of its graceful play
    beside its soft brown mother
    in the morning of its day,
a scene transcending even the sight of
ripped-out guts for he knew the truth that
    death ruins no bloom;
    beauty however short
    outweighs the waiting tomb,
but one day at somebody's smelly poultry
farm some mud-splattered rooster attacked
some turkey twice its size, bug-eyed and
blood-red-wattled, which beak-clutched the
chicken's neck and shook and dumped
it in the dirt and poultry poop, and
the chicken—it didn't die—picked itself
up and wobbled off, and ever after he
couldn't quite get that out of his
mind, that image went on fluttering in
his brain, that really
shook him.

All of a sudden

All of a sudden at the breakfast
table as he read in the morning
newspaper of starvation somewhere
he noticed that his eyes began
dripping tears, and he felt compelled to
get up and put on his suit and shirt and
tie and go down to the local Food
Bank and volunteer to dole out
food to poor people who otherwise
wouldn't have enough to eat, and
as he did that he noticed that
his eyes again began dripping
tears, and as more people came to
get food, more tears dripped from
his eyes until the water became a
flood all over his suit and shirt and
tie and they told him he had to quit
volunteering there and go see a
psychologist in order to get control of
his emotions, and he did so and learned
that he shouldn't take things so
personally and didn't have to take on the
burdens of the world and should care only
about what he could, and so he went
back to the Food Bank a couple of
hours on Saturdays and thereafter seemed
able to resume having breakfast and
reading his morning paper just fine.

At eighty-four

At eighty-four in the basement he
slogged through old boxes in
which he had stashed his
life: letters, photos, some
documents, but reading them made
his experience seem different than
he remembered, yet he still believed that
somewhere in the boxes something
would surely make sense, so he slaved on
under the light of the basement's naked
bulb, rummaging—old bound diaries,
the glue loosening in their backs—
they ought to remind him of what
was significant, and he read and
remembered this and that and
the sense things made at the time and
he began to get sleepy and
he dozed off and the light seemed
dim, inadequate, and a journal fell
from his hands and in the shadows
nearby a mouse waited to get at
the glue.

No car crash

No car crash, no road kill, no
dead deer in the ditch, no holes in
the pavement, nothing on this familiar
road that he drove daily to work and
back to account for the sudden
sensation he felt of wild fear, but
despite a bright sun, white clouds, and
a quiet blue sky, he felt he should
slow, stop, get out and run, but then
as usual he reached the ordinary
bridge that spanned the ordinary
river, and as he drove onto it he
realized that it arched before him just
enough that he could not see the other
side, and right then and there he
stopped, U-turned on the bridge, drove
back off, then pulled to the side of
the road, stopped and waited and
watched, not knowing what would
happen, not knowing what would
come, not able to see beyond the
bridge's arch, watched the sun go
down beyond the arch and wondered
whether he could ever cross the
bridge again.

It began when one day

It began when one day he reached for
the door knob and the knob seemed not
there and the door itself seemed away,
apart, and he backed to a chair and sat
down, and then one day he looked out
a window and the window seemed three
inches thick making things look indistinct and
unreachable and far away, and he had to
go lie down for a while, and then on
another day he looked outside at the
fall colors of the trees and realized that
they had become just as distant and
indistinct as the thickened window had
made the outdoors look, but this time he
refused to back away and try to
recover; instead he mustered up self-
mastery and squinted his eyes into the
closest focus he could achieve and then
he marched toward the closest grove of
trees, hands outstretched to touch them, if
he could just touch them; but then he
stopped, he sat down, he knew then that
he could not even touch the yellowing
grass on which he now found himself
sitting.

That morning

That morning he awoke and saw that an
asteroid would smash the earth, he saw that it
would, no one else saw, no one else agreed that
it would, he alone, and it made him mad, not
that no one else agreed, but that it would
smash, because if it did, nothing would matter and
everything would be gone, and
hardly time enough remained to love enough to
make up for that, time to hover in a shelter and
say, "I love you, I love you all," while you
realized that no shelter could be adequate, but
"I love you" would be the one comfort, the one
defiance, the one real meaningful thing before the
meteor hit, and it made him mad to think that the
asteroid might put an end even to that, even for
those who went through entire lives of
love thinking there was no asteroid, and he
thought that the asteroid wouldn't matter, at
least not so much, if someone, after it hit, could
go on saying "I love you"—that would matter and
anyway what else could matter in a world about
to be incinerated by an asteroid, even if
before it hit no one was able to see it, and
no one would be left to whom it could
be said.

Sitting in the river

Sitting in the river, feeling it
move caressingly around him as if
he hardly were there, and feeling the
breeze, too, as if ten hundred invisible
chickadees had embraced him with their
caressing wings, and the light, too, would
float over his shoulders like a warm but
tingling effervescence, and nothing wrong—
can you imagine how he felt?—So
he never left there, he never moved again, and
he stayed put exactly as he was under the
caressing stream, the embracing breeze, the
effervescent light because something obviously
loved him, and then he realized that if he
never knew where the river came from or
where the breeze came from or where the
light—what did it matter what he
didn't know, he knew that he could be
impervious to flood, to storm, to fire, if
he just remembered, if he just understood, if
he just recognized that somebody, even if
it all came to an end, that's what he must try
to persuade himself of, that somebody must
actually, and so he stayed there regardless
because he knew that someday, yes, eventually,
undoubtedly, if he could just keep staying there,
somebody would surely, it was all going to be
all right.

The teddy bear sat

The teddy bear sat on the shelf, though
not really, because, a shape of stuffed
fluff, it required that someone place it, he or
his mother, to whom it had first been
given, and later left to him to inherit, all
of which is to say he saw it there daily, staring
at him out of its remaining glass eye, the
other having been lost years earlier, he knew
not where or how, and what did it matter
anyway how many eyes an old scruffy
stuffed animal toy still had out of which to
stare at him, which it actually didn't
do because it wasn't a being but only an
inanimate thing, as he well knew, so
why didn't he pull out the remaining
eye, then it wouldn't, but he understood that
it still would, that the holes where the
eyes had been would stare out at him even
though he knew their staring was all in his
own mind, which made him afraid just to
throw the old bear out in the trash because
then, he knew, he would still see it staring at
him out of his own mind, and he did not
know how to tear it out of there, how to
stop things that didn't matter, couldn't
see, and seemingly had no end—how to
stop them from staring at him.

He had reached

He had reached about the middle when he
noticed his pen had begun to leak, which
didn't matter much, this being only a
draft, except for the irritation of having to
stop to do something about the pen's
leaking, but no matter what he did to
fix it, it kept leaking, in fact, it now
leaked all over the page and even
threatened to obliterate what he had
written, which he didn't want to lose, so
he stopped writing and stopped trying to
fix the pen and took another sheet of
paper and another pen and began to
copy what remained of what he had
previously written, only to find that the
new pen also leaked, in fact leaked even
more than the old one, leaving the new
sheet a wet ink-saturated mass, which
made him think this must be just in his
mind, so he asked his wife to come see if
she thought his pen was leaking, and
she came and she said, "No, no leakage," the
pen looked fine, so he tried to resume
writing, then stopped, that's when he
remembered, it came back to him then
that he didn't have a wife.

She wanted to listen

She wanted to listen to the song, the
one that kept glowing in her mind, the
one they were playing that night when
the boy danced with her, the dreamy
handsome boy, but the pastor came to
talk to her about God's love in the
afterlife, and how He would be
waiting, and the pastor changed
her calendar, the one with the *Famous
Paintings of Jesus,* so that it would
show the right month, but she didn't
care which month it was, nor which
picture of Jesus, because in her head she
had a picture of that boy, and she just
wanted to hear that song, and nothing
else mattered except, perhaps, the
half-cup of weak coffee they allowed
her each morning—it smelled so nice!

PART THREE

Once he saw

Once he saw, he knew—he joined the
class in which the old woodsman with
the crevassed face as cracked as the
surface of a Great North pond taught
senior citizens to make their own
snowshoes, and the beauty of
those symmetrically curved, brightly
polished strips of wood between which
he learned to weave thick cords into
exquisitely intricate patterns—"Here,
pull it tighter, keep the pattern," the
old man would say—and out of the
intensely wild weaving the pattern would
emerge, grow, and fulfill itself within
the embracing wood strips, and he
kept stretching, tightening, and
loving the patterns until he finished his
first shoes, and then he started his second
pair, and then went on to the third, and
made different shapes of snowshoes to
meet every kind of treacherous surface and
paid no attention when they said he should
stop, that he couldn't keep coming and
making, but he did keep coming and
making, with ever more perfect
patterns elaborately laced because
he knew one could never have too
many snowshoes, no, nor even have
snowshoes enough.

The night became

The night became so black that
he could see only cloudily within
it, and increasingly it closed in about
him, at first like water, something
thickly liquid through which he
could move, but only with
effort, resisting him even while
it seemed to seek him, and then
it gradually became more solid, almost
—it seemed crazy to say it—like
gelatin, still giving way but nearly
impossible to move through, then
harder still until he could feel it all
about him as if the universe had
congealed, and then he could not
move at all, but he knew that the
universe did not work that way, that
the night existed only as the
absence of the sun, and that if
he did not panic but just held
still until the dawn, the
darkness probably would not,
could not crush him.

He sat there

He sat there in the dark, the
door closed, the light off, staying within
the confines of the water closet, attempting to
defecate, thinking about how they used to
say, "Appearances are everything," which
is why he had closed the door, turned
off the light, and confined himself alone in
the dark, for this act that he was doing should
not be seen, even by himself, lest
barbarism threaten those who believed that
life could be more than sitting alone for
all one's days in the cramping confines of
a water closet with the light out and
the door shut, defecating.

What sense did it make

What sense did it make, this coagulation of
molecules into the particular density called
wood that composed the desk at which he
sat, he, an aggregation of mutations including
what his mind called a mind, capable of
differentiating among densities, and in
fact insisting on them whether or not reality
actually had differentiability outside the
need of this same mind for finding it, for
finding pattern, order, sense, which seemed to
help his kind of aggregation survive in a
world of snakes, hailstones, car accidents, and
cancers, the latter seeming to be the
body doing in itself, a weirdly aggregated
body that required a skeletal system, an immune
system, a vascular system, a gastro-intestinal
system, a reproductive system, a nervous
system—especially and most strangely a
nervous system, the system by which he
recognized just how strange all of his
aggregation was, just as strange as that wood
desk, those snakes, those hail stones, those
car accidents, those cancers, and this made his
pattern-seeking mind wonder why he wasn't
created as just a single, solitary, unitary,
impermeable, indestructible thing, but the
explanation for that came when he realized that
the simple perfection one might expect a god to
create, or a scientist, would have no need for a
mind, especially for one that wondered why it
had one.

As he was making

As he was making quite delightful love with
his wife it occurred to him that one could
be happy yet feel that life stank, that the
world stank, because, while it put a
reproductive premium on making love it also
killed, maimed, drowned, burned, bombed,
murdered, cancer-struck, injured, crazed, etc., so
much of what love-making produced, that
is, forms of life, such as birds, rabbits, and
people, along with hagfish, rattlesnakes, and
wolves; so maybe the trick was to make love all
the time without reproducing, but
then life would soon come to a halt, and so
he didn't bring this up to his wife but got up the
next morning and ate an omelet and thought about
how delicious the omelet was and instead of
sex maybe one should constantly eat omelets, thus
pleasurably avoiding reproduction, especially
because of what omelets were made of, though
chickens would just as soon that the planet killed all
humans, because that, too, would increase
happiness, that would make life not stink so much
for chickens.

What he thought

What he thought about it was that
he need not think about it, that
was one way out, but instead he should
think whatever it stimulated to come into
his—; but do not finish any—; do not
let—; but then he saw that even as
he refused to say what not to do, he had
done just that, done that because—
no, do not let "becauses," allow nothing
reductive, or it will become merely a
prune, a salted slug, a proper poem; but
if he did not write something out with
statements and sense, no one would
know what not to do; yet did he need to
go that far to avoid boiling all of it down
into a kind of gimcrackery, avoid what
his steam-hammer of a mind might do to
it, when maybe all he had to do was just
never to define
it?

How wonderful!

How wonderful!—the idea of a Celebration of
Greatness, the entire city taking part, and
all over the people had begun to prepare, and
he, too, as he sat there in the front row in the
auditorium with the chorus to practice singing the
Great Anthem—but as they started singing, he
suddenly realized he didn't know the music, could
not reach the high notes or the low, never had
learned a part, alto or tenor, and had to get
away, duck out when the others, their eyes all
on the flailing conductor, would not see him down
on his hands and knees, moving up the aisle, through
the doorway, out of the auditorium, into the
street, into the crowd, where no one likely would
recognize him, and once outside, he took off as fast as
he could, farther away from the auditorium, until he
felt he had lost himself among all the people who
were making preparations for the Celebration—
the carpenters at work building and the
artists painting and the sculptors sculpting and the
dancers rehearsing and the poets composing and the
orators declaiming and the bakers baking and the
sausage-makers stuffing and the brewers brewing and
everyone working, crowds so busy, and
everything so colorful as the florists decorated the
city with wreaths and sprigs and sprays and
multicolored blooms, and along the streets the
various groups prepared their elaborate floats for
the Parade of Greatness, and then
he began to feel safe, even stopping now and
again to gaze at this spectacle, marveling at
the skills of all these people and their energies, how
gleefully they shouted to each other as they worked, and
what a hubbub they made, jostling and crowding in
the streets, until finally he reached the end of
the city, the farthest edge, where he could sit on a
stone bench and look down from the city wall into the
void beyond, the empty silence, which seemed such a
contrast with the hustle and bustle within the city, and
as he turned back to watch, he thought—which

group should he join to help get ready for the
Day of Greatness?—and he
sat there and thought about it, and
he enjoyed thinking about it as he looked at
this activity and that and imagined what fun it
was all going to be, and he sat there, not worrying any
more, but sat in delight, admiring all the
magnificent preparations for the city's soon-to-
come, gloriously grand Festival of Greatness, sat
there where no one would think to look down on or
even to recognize
him.

They shut him out

They shut him out with speculation that
either he'd gone crazy, succumbed to
neurosis, or taken to drinking too
much, all because he had loaded up a
little wagon—a kid's wagon—with a
thermos, a lunch pail, pencils, and a
ream or two of paper and headed over
the hill behind his house, saying he was
going to go as far as he could beyond the
woods and see as far as he could
see, so when he didn't come back by
nightfall, somebody called the game
wardens, who went looking for
him, thinking he might have broken
a leg or encountered a bear, but
all they found was the wagon, and
they never did find him, no, they were
never able to go that far beyond
the woods.

The damned cork

The damned cork came out when
he tipped over the bottle of
wine, the last bottle of wine on
earth, tipped it over *accidentally*, a
pure accident, not some subconsciously
demanded impulse, he was sure of
that because, perverting as
his subconscious might be, it would
never compel him to tip over and
spill out all the wine from the last
bottle of it on earth, never, and
anyway, spilling it took more than
tipping over the bottle, it also
required failing to get the cork in
tight, which means two acts of
perversion by his subconscious would
have been required to spill the last
wine, but why didn't he get the cork in
tight, and why didn't he take adequate
care to avoid tipping over the bottle, and
why did it have to be the last wine left
on earth?—maybe that was the bigger
question, the overarching question, the
one that threatened a more perverse
answer than his subconscious could
provide: why did it have to be the last
bottle of wine on earth?

She sat and fidgeted

She sat and fidgeted because of the
mushiness of the pear, and they
bought pears so infrequently, almost
never, and, she began to feel
tears coming because they never
got it right even when they did buy
pears because they didn't know
when the fruit was just right, not
overripe and mushy or green and
hard, and she begged them to
get it right saying that you had to
know how to feel pears to
tell when to eat them, and she
knew how, so why couldn't they
learn or let her do it—that was
it, let her do it, buy pears green, bring
them to her, let her feel them each
morning to see whether they were
yet ready to eat, and then she could
tell everybody and they would all
enjoy pears and everybody could be so
happy and she wouldn't have to
long for perfect pears so much
and be so disappointed even
when they bought pears—why did
it have to be so difficult to get
this one thing right?—why did
pears, which could be so sweet, so
delicious, have to be so incredibly
difficult?!

PART FOUR

If he stared

If he stared at it long enough, he
feared, it would no longer be a fragment from
something grand, an architectural
artifact, fallen down or torn off a
cathedral, part of a great construction of
mankind's, and no longer would it be a
sculpted figure, carved with great care, even
with love, by someone anonymous but
skilled, even holy, who had turned it into the
figure of a saint in sandals with flowing
robes under a long cloak, with curled
hair falling evenly down to his shoulders, with
one hand holding a cross and the other
upright, the fingers pressed together, and on
his face a full beard and full-of-message
eyes and a small mouth, and if he just went on
staring at it, the holy and powerful being would
cease to be a symbol, and the hands would
cease to make an accepting, beneficent gesture, and
the gentle, unencumbering cloak would flow
away, and the assuring, blesséd face addressing
him as if infused with quiet joy would become
just chisel marks, and he would see that what he
really saw within and behind all the thousands of
years of grand, skilled, gifted, blesséd, holy, even
loving constructs would be a piece of
blank stone, or maybe something even
more inscrutable, maybe something he
would not be able to see
at all.

What a breeze

"What a breeze of wind that was," the
man said, and his wife said, "Yes, it
stormed some all right, and came up so
fast and then blew like doom," and then
they described how it blew their lawn
furniture, lawn mower, garden tools, snow
blower, barbeque grill, croquet mallets, and
trash cans into a meld of metal and
wood, all mangled together up the
side of the hill behind their house, and
how tree limbs littered the woods on the
hill and how blown-out window glass and
ripped-off roof tiles wound up all over the
township next to theirs, "But also," the
newspaper reporter asked, "what about
your children?" and she said, "Yes, it
caught them out in the yard and
we don't know where they may be, and
the forest ranger said they'd keep an
eye out for them, but, I don't know, we
may never see them again," and the
man added, "Yes, but you can't let bad
luck get you down, you have to take
things as they come, take things
just as they come."

Immediately he recognized

Immediately he recognized it as a
metaphor, a metaphoric force, this
crack opening up in the driveway in
front of his house, a slow opening at
first, apparently just the kind of
crack that one sees often in the
ground toward the end of a cold
winter, which worried him only
when the crack kept expanding, kept
deepening, until he had to drive
around it to get out and then back
into his property, and even then it
didn't stop widening and also
lengthening, coming almost up to
his house, where, if it kept on
opening, it would form a chasm, an
abyss, and would swallow up his
house, his family, even himself—all
he cared about would disappear into
the bottom of the abyss—but then, just
as it seemed to happen, the chasm
began to decline, grew smaller, became
gradually shorter and narrower, and
eventually withdraw, vanished, closed
up, and it never opened again, which
made him wonder—was it a
metaphor?—or did it do all this just to
show that it could?

They had always told him

They had always told him to fight
back, and he remembered how
they had told him to do it, so
every morning he set aside time to
lie in bed and listen to the song
birds chirp in their celebrations of
the reappearing sun, and each after-
noon he took time to ramble through
his garden to smell the roses, inhaling
their soothing perfume, and each
evening he devoted a half hour to
standing under the stars, watching
their tiny brilliant bright lights, which
looked like millions of minute
fires were trying to break through the
dark, and as he did all this he told him-
self that every blink of a star and
every emanation of a rose and every
chirp of a bird constituted a resisting
act, a fighting back, and so, too, did
that notion itself, and so did every
other kind of supposition he could
think of to possibly persuade himself
that beauty ruled the world.

At last

At last the explanation of
everything had come to him as clear as
could be, so clear that he wondered how
he could have failed to see it before, had
gone so many years without seeing it, until
all at once one night in a magnificently
sweet dream with a bolt of lightning and
a gigantic thunder burst the explanation
came, so he got out of bed, grabbed a
pen and pad of paper, and, without
washing, dressing or even having tea, he
began to write what he could remember—
the answer to everything!—the gist of
it at least, if, in his waking state, with
pen ready, he could just remember, but he
soon realized that he could not, not even a
bit, which seemed so odd because the
explanation had so filled his mind that he
had felt compelled to wake up and write it
down, and now—but never mind, he
recognized what he could do, which was
get back into the dream, that is, get back
in bed, close his eyes, and return to
sleep, and then stay there, get the lightning
back, and see all as clearly as before, the
explanation of everything would return and
this time stay with him if he could just get
back to sleep.

Be careful

"Be careful," she advised him about his
fascination with the wild turkey, the
one with an injured leg, useless, pulled
up beneath as it hopped along trying to
keep with the flock that daily came out
of the woods, over the brow of the
hill behind their house, down to their
bird feeders, eager for seeds; but each
day the turkey reappeared, seeming even
more miraculous as it survived coyotes,
foxes, bears, and others that culled the
weak and wounded, and each day it
returned, limping along, vulnerable in
its one-leggedness, yet relentlessly
keeping up, its life seeming to assert—
"No," she warned, "do not make that
maimed bird, that poor creature, a
symbol, a metaphor;" but how could
he not see in it the force of life, the
power of the desire to persist—"No,"
she repeated, "you are trying to
reduce it to fit the fixed enclosure of
your intellect," but he would not
heed, and even told himself how the
sight expanded his mind, made him
see the magic, the struggle to put off the
end while demonstrating possibility—
"That's what I feared," she said, "that
you would run after it, chase it
down, take it captive, and bind the dying
thing within the airtight confines of
some cozy poem."

At first

At first, he didn't believe it himself, so
he spent days checking and double-
checking everything but the results kept
coming up the same, and they had to
be right, the study was too controlled, the
sample too extensive, the time too
lengthy for doubt, but still he kept
putting off an announcement, even to his
own colleagues, who watched him come
and go out of the lab, refusing access to
anyone else, hiding all the data, saying
nothing, until they started wondering
what he could be doing, because more
time had passed than anyone would
need to compile and check and issue a
report, and they wondered whether he
himself had succumbed, become a
victim of the affliction under
study, contracted its debilitating
effects, but the more they tried to
find out, the more he put them off and
would not even tell them why, for how
could he, how could he be the one to
announce to the world that the
study showed that everyone surveyed in
it had the affliction, suggesting, making
it almost certain, that the affliction was
endemic to everybody.

Just stay calm

Just stay calm, that was the thing he
told himself, the thing he tried to
keep uppermost in his mind as
time went on, stay calm, because
calm could be better than courage, it
could be the ultimate courage, to
be unaffected by whatever happened, to
reject being disconcerted, unhinged, or
debilitated by anything, to sit vacant-
minded in a cave and stay that way when
it caved in, even to bask in disaster, to
suck up whatever came in the
way of pain, because if he could do
that, they would say, he is sane, so
unflappable, so admirably in
control, so attuned to normality that
he finds it natural, for of course even
above courage, even above calm, the
key would be control, wouldn't it?—
yes, calm, courage, and control would
equal wisdom, and he knew that
because wisdom always seemed to
come in words that alliterate, always
seemed to come in words that
one could easily remember, even
through you couldn't say them in, say,
the suffocation of a caved-in cave, or
any other real emergency.

He liked to sit

He liked to sit on the stoop in front of
his house and watch the evening darken,
the sun go down, the stars emerge, the
moon glide, except this got to be harder
because the stoop began to list, tilting
increasingly until he had to lean the
opposite way and eventually hang on to
the stoop to keep from sliding off, and
a walk around it to inspect turned up no
explanation, which meant some unseen
natural phenomenon must be at
work, such as a sinkhole or tectonic
shift, so he just adjusted, hanging on and
leaning to keep from sliding, he
adjusted as one should do when faced
with change, and as the world went
careening like a miss-shot marble into the
night, and the lights of stars kept
trying to realign, he could see that
leaning farther and farther to keep from
sliding off his perch was the natural and
even normal (if slightly uncomfortable)
thing to do.

So when they told her

So when they told her that her
best friend of many decades had
died, she felt surprised because
she thought that friend had died years
ago, so many had already gone, three
or four a year it had seemed for a
while, one got used to the end of
friends, one didn't give them much
thought anymore, the tears seemed
to quit coming, the memories lost
meaning, each departure took with
it another sequence of events from
a past that became increasingly
less real until even what she could
remember little mattered, and even
the new friends here in the home got
carried out from time to time and
other new ones appeared to the
point that she quit even trying to
keep track but instead enjoyed
the flowers that also appeared now
and then with labels that said *In
Memoriam* to one or another
name she was not sure she really
recognized, but the flowers—the
flowers often amazed her with
their bright beauty, sometimes
immaculately white, sometimes
orange or red, sometimes a hurt
purple, and when some bouquets of
flowers faded it didn't really
matter because more soon
appeared, usually quite soon, and
always she found them quite
beautiful.

PART FIVE

Magnificently huge

Magnificently huge, this lily, which
is why he felt he should save it, nurture
it, defy indifference to its beauty, so
he carefully potted it and took it
inside where he could keep it relatively
warm, water it, give it plant food, and
when it seemed to wane anyway he
bought some silvery nail polish which
he dabbed over darkening spots on its
leaves, so that eventually it regained
its magnificent look, unblemished and
undefiled, and then for a few days he
looked at it, just looked and smiled, and
then he got out his Bible and began to
read to it, the Psalms, over and over, the
embalming Psalms, and when he saw that
its leaves began to wilt anyway he
bought some silvery metallic paint and
covered the entire plant so that it
gleamed with even greater
magnificence, made him proud of his
ingenuity, and made him think—what
else could he possibly do of more
importance than this, to enable one
lily of the valley to go on mocking the
scythe, that made him feel a bit like,
well, why not say it, why not?

After his wife

After his wife died and most of the
guys he joined for morning coffee down
at the One-Stop, he persuaded
himself—"Why not?"—and so
he had the big bed hauled out and a little
one brought in and he found the old
quilt in the attic and the old curtains that
his mother had made, and he had the
room repainted the way she had
painted it, and he found in antique
stores a short chest-of-drawers and some
other furniture resembling the
furnishings he remembered, and he even
located some bright, crocheted throw
rugs she had made, and the more
success he had with this the more he
said to himself—"And why not?"—
but the next part was tougher, finding
the same old toys, the metal soldiers, the
stuffed animals, the blocks and tops and
all, or at least some similar ones, and of
course the storybooks, which eventually
he did find, battered old copies but
still full of the characters who had
fascinated him in those days when he
could feel that he entered what he
read, that they were real, and that
he knew them personally and could be
with them—Pinocchio, Hansel and
Gretel, Robin Hood, Raggedy
Ann, Wonderland's Alice, Uncle
Wiggly, Winnie-the-Pooh, and all the
rest—and when he had retrieved them all,
he closed the door, closed it tight and
put on some pajamas and got in the
bed, and felt how cozy and complete and
full of comfort it was as he opened one of
the books and began to read, "Once
upon a time...."

The older he got

The older he got, the more he
noticed that things changed on the
walls of his house, that all of
his framed works of art became
mirrors, and each of his windows
did also, until all about
him mirrors reflected—what?—
him?—but each mirror changed each
time he looked at it, until he
realized that they reflected how he
saw himself, which seemed more
absurd the older he became, for he
sometimes imagined himself a wise
sage, a knight in shining armor, an
applauded scholar, a victorious
general, a celebrated statesman—
the only end to this would be his
end, but where in the mirrors was his
beginning, where was the child who
first learned to tell himself such
tales, or the ordinary adult who mucked
through life like everyone else, keeping
himself afloat on shadows of
possibility, but he could also make those
images, too, appear, because apparently
whatever he supposed himself to be would
appear in a mirror, so why not fill the
mirrors with whatever he might
want, maybe even with the image of a
great truth-seeker who never ever
would tell himself lies?

It troubled him

It troubled him to feel he could not
break through, peck past the egg
shell of his skull into the limitless
all-about, but instead had to
skulk along the overgrown mazes of
his brain to their blind ends, keeping
his synapses crackling but for
what?—watching all the busy
minds about him creating nests to
rest in, some achieving comfort through
inverted telescopes, others
making a virtue of indifference, still
others painting sunshine on the
undersides of clouds, and all fearing
nothing so much as cracks in their
imaginings, while he sat in a
tree, eschewing cheek-rouge, his
tiny eyes deprived of lids, hoping to
detect a crack in the atmosphere through
which to see what beyondness might
really look like before the painter of
creation could take up a trowel and
smooth it all over again.

Try games

Try games, they told him, Rummy, Old
Maid, Hearts, Bridge, Cribbage, whatever
he could give full concentration, that was
the trick, along with gaining strength from
social bonding, so he bought a pack of
cards, learned to shuffle and deal, invited
in some friends—
    aces, deuces, this is fun,
    round the table, watch them fall,
    take your chances, everyone,
and soon he had developed some real
skill, learned to keep the card count in his
mind, learned to judge which cards to
keep, and which discard, sat for hours sipping
lemonade, joked with friends as win-streaks
rose and fell, felt the thrill when the right
card came up and his hand filled, victorious—
    clubs and diamonds, why ask more
    than well-honed skill, bit of luck,
    and friends of congenial temperature,
yes, if only he could just keep playing games,
that was the trick, if he could just keep on
playing.

As he sat

As he sat in the waiting room he
couldn't help noticing how it
stayed full of patients and how
some talked with others and some
didn't and now and then someone
would moan or groan and a
doctor or nurse would come out and
administer a pill or a shot or give the
moaner a new magazine or turn up the
TV, which they always kept on, and
now and then a patient would
fall over and someone would come
put the patient on a gurney and
roll it out and some patients told
jokes and some prayed and that's the
way it was, and he kept thinking—how
did he get in here?—but deep down
inside him something kept telling
him that no matter what, he really
did not want to get out.

They said he was

They said he was failing to see; he
should look at the tulips, how
beautiful they were, so he looked and
he did see—bright red, shining
yellow, stately purple, petals so
silky, shapes chalice-like, all
sprightly, luminescent, glowing under
the beams of warm sun and drifts of
white clouds, embodiments of
wonder and delight,
    O life, O light, O deep regenerative power,
    Thy glory reigns however brief thy hour!
                          and their
admirers were right, he should keep his
eyes on them, and he resolved always
to do it, just focus, concentrate on the
beauty of the tulips under the sun and
sky, just keep his mind on their
miraculous glow, worship that glow and
give no thought to anything else, keep
all the rest of it out, and then—
maybe then, eventually there would
be no "rest of it."

They told him such

They told him such sights make
life worthwhile, so he stopped to
watch when the ruby-throated
hummingbird with its shimmering
green back suspended its whirly-
gigging wings long enough to be
seen, sitting on a feeder, dipping its
long, needle-like beak into the
opening, extracting the sweet
nutritious syrup until you would
think the little bird would
burst, but then it whizzed away as
fast as it had come, its translucent
wings beating so quickly you could
hardly see their structure, and he
thought it must all be in the *ings*—
the shimmerings and extractings and
whizzings—and as long as living
things had *ings*, why should he have
such doubts, why shouldn't he just
let his mind go on humming and
flapping as if it, too, had the power to
get somewhere.

It amazed him how

It amazed him how, when he woke up in
the night, his mind could scare him with
thoughts of what he could not control or
prevent or survive, so he felt
anxieties, fears, as if something had
arisen around him in the dark, grabbed
him, and threatened to fling him over the
edge—of what he did not know, which
was the scariest thing about it, but then the
next morning, he would wake up to find
his mind laughing, scorning the night's
anxieties, dismissing them as bogies that
arise out of being only partly awake and
still subject to the domain of dreams, things
that, in the light of being fully awake, must
be seen as silly, which was even
scarier yet, not because his mind assailed
itself in this contradictory way, but because
he found himself wondering—how many
minds did he have?

Where did the cat go?

Where did the cat go? Where? Since
she fell once, twice, they wouldn't
let her get up and go look, the one
with orange stripes, white paws, and
thick fur that liked to sit on her lap and
be petted and would purr, purr, and—
where was . . . ?
    All day long it bedded there
    on her lap as she rocked her chair,
    and time laid down and rested too
    and turned so soft and warm and true,
and to stop her constant repeating, they
wheeled her into the TV room and hoped
she'd be distracted as the people on the
screen talked at her, smiled, made
jokes, told news, and kept on about
food and clothes and weather and
winning ways, but she knew they
were not real, just make believe, pictures
on a screen, and not even the program they
found for her about cats, all the various
kinds and colors prancing for judges in a
cat contest, not even that kept her quiet for
long, just pictures—she stretched
towards them, reached out her
fingers, touched, but the pictures kept
going as if she hadn't, as if she were
not even there, as if no one kept saying
to them—*Where is my cat?*

PART SIX

Sports can be

Sports can be absorbing, they told
him; try sports, so he found his
baseball, bat, and mitt, and went
down the street to the beautiful
park where the town had laid out the
diamond for the games by little-
leaguers, and he stood at home
plate and tossed up the ball and
smacked it as hard as he could into
the air, then, grabbing his
mitt, he ran out under the ball as
fast as he could and caught it, and
even though he fell down in the
process, it all felt good, the
lunging of his muscles into the
swing of the bat, the satisfying
smack of the bat's sweet spot on
the ball, the steep rise of the
ball high into the air, the
stretching of his legs as he ran to
get beneath it, the smack of the
ball into his mitt, his hanging
onto it even as he found him-
self off-balance diving onto the
infield grass—all so
absorbing and satisfying just
as they said, so he did it over and
over until at last the feeling
filled him that the world permitted
all the at-bats you wanted and
never would put you out.

They told him

They told him, why don't you do the
obvious like everybody else and stay in
some satisfying subjective state of
mind such as scientists do when they
search for knowledge, like artists
do when they express truth, beauty, or
whatever, like theologians do when
they seek understanding of the gods, and
so he went out into a cave, wearing only
an animal skin, and made a fire using
flint to strike sparks into dry leaves and
charred a piece of wood so that it would
make marks on a smooth earthen
wall and did his best to capture in a
few broad strokes the spirit of
giant lions, hook-horned bison, and
fragile fleeing deer, and he
kneeled down to the sight of those
spirits and begged to be one with
them and not an isolated creature in
a place where fires went out, walls
caved in, and animals either threatened
mayhem or kept out of sight, but
then he thought, what happens if I
put a human figure up there with a
bright light emanating from him, so
he did it and it glowed, it radiated, and
it kept doing that, kept up that wonderful
glow until the fire went out.

Illusion

"Illusion," someone said as she told of
the red-chested robin who hopped all
alone across close-cropped grass in
her mowed yard—a hop, a stop, then
a cock of the head, then the
sequence again, yard fenced by
flowers, orange poppies, white
daisies, pink peonies, red roses—and
she did not try to make too much of
all this, just watched in stillness until
someone said, "The scene is at best only
molecules roiling, it's fool's gold of the
mind entranced with its own power to
make patterns, and the colors you seem to
love are but lengths of waves of light
insinuating through your retinas so even
in daylight you move in a kind of irremediable
dark," but the pattern her mind made seemed
sufficient, a credit to her intellect, green
grass, bright flowers, and a pert bird, yes,
she let them all into her garden, the one with
the high brick wall around it and
no weeds.

She kept putting

She kept putting out grain every
day and deer came, also wild
turkeys, crows, jays, and
songbirds, and at night
raccoons and possums to
her open compost pile, and
twice even black bears behind
her house, tipping her bird
feeders into their mouths, and
everybody told her, "You must not
feed wild animals"; the game
wardens told her, and her
neighbors, and even members of
her congregation said the
animals would tear up her
yard, eat her garden, become
dependent on her, and "feeding
them will only expand the
numbers to be fed," they said; "leave
them to God";
and that's when she knew she
had to keep feeding them, not
because she necessarily wanted
more but because she felt frightened as
she realized what her neighbors, the
game wardens, and God had in mind
for such creatures.

And the sun

And the sun shone and
and the clouds puffed and
the quaint sparkling town waited
in the distance, its every happy
inhabitant seemed to call, and the
smooth, open road showed the
way, invited, and so he
took up his favorite unbroken
crayons, and he colored the
sun orange-red, the
clouds bright-white, the
town warm-brown, the
road glittering gold, and
the full hay-laden fields gleaming
summer green, and then all glowed in
color
and everyone waited as he
looked, loving, and hoping to
find the color that would make it all
real.

Conversing he discovered

Conversing he discovered himself in
an endless ocean with others, all
treading water in panic while tossing
each other lifelines—ropes with
buoys at their ends—each
speaker tossing one, then another, each
getting one back, then another, so that
when the tossing ended each had the
feeling of having been repeatedly
saved, but then in the lull, he and the
rest felt drifting in different
directions until almost out of each
other's sight, starting to
sink, whereupon everyone began
again tossing lifelines, flipping
them all about, enabling each of the
speakers to pull closer once more and
tread water better until the process
repeated, repeated, all of which
seemed silly except that he couldn't
stop for fear that if he did he would
drown.

Meadowlarks and mourning

(for Gene George, 1942-2012)

Meadowlarks and mourning
doves, tugging wind and drifting
snow, cattle down by the pasture
stream, kittens born in the
granary, swallows nesting in the
barn's eaves, chickens scratching after
corn, and now all gone, even the old
white house where the relatives had
so often come for dinner after
church, the uncle who could
wrestle the fiddle, and the one
who brought a candy sack, and the
aunt who banged the piano and
sang, and the one who had bags of
spools and blocks and plastic
horses and tiny trucks, and the grand-
mother whose kitchen steamed and
the grandfather whose humble voice
intoned the blessing—now gone as
if none had ever been, and for
once he thought he could believe in
ghosts, oh not that any now would
appear, but ghosts all the same—the
ones that those who now had disappeared
must have been.

Freezing wind blew

Freezing wind blew a rusty
shopping cart across a crumbling
parking lot, an empty cart, wobbly
on cracked plastic wheels over
asphalt fractured beyond
repair, and suddenly, as he
watched, terrified, up to the
wreck of the cart came a yellow
ragged cat shivering, sniffing,
searching, crazed with wild
eyes and claws, eager to find
anything.

The assembled bones

The assembled bones of the
great whale arching across the
room, vertebrae strung
together white as chalk, and
behind, in the cornered
window, a potted ficus
tree tossing up leaves, yellow
and green, full of outside
sun, and this ensemble of
dead bones, live leaves, and
vivifying shine began, in the
eyes of his mind, to explode as
if the instability of such a
juxtaposition were too much, as
if its incompatibilities were too
true, as if at any moment the
fleshless bones of the
whale would whirl off to
reassemble in a dark corner of
the otherwise empty room, and
the leaves would loose and
spiral and drift until all were in
small, unnoticeable piles, and
someone would come in the
aftermath and pull the curtain on
the sun.

They're down in the cellar

"They're down in the cellar," she
said and she kept saying it until they
asked "Who," and she said if
they'd take her down there she'd
show them, and they said, "Well," and
they went away for a while, but
then she got one of them, and so they
said, "All right, we'll take you down
there, and then you'll go lie
down in your bed and stay there, and
who do you think is down there any
way?"
    Celia was a little girl, we played,
      we played,
    and Harold was a boy I knew,
      when I kissed he stayed,
    until his mother came to get him,
      oh how she did scold!
    And Celia came in too but never
      told.
"See, there's nobody here," and then
they turned off the lights and said
why didn't I go up and get back
into bed, and I went back to bed and I
thought about it and I said that they
were there in the cellar, and they said, "No,
they're dead, and I could not play with
them anymore."

PART SEVEN

In the yellow-bright flicker

In the yellow-bright flicker of
the fire he seemed to see the
pulse rising, falling back, rising
again against the crouching
dark, the fire whose warmth gave
comfort and whose light gave
sight so that one did not have to
dwell in chill or flounder in
sinister shadow—"keep on," he
said to himself, "just keep this
going"—so he heaped more
stripped branches, broken bark, and
brittle leaves into the flames until
sparks flew high in the air as
if the fire were making its own
stars out of dead debris discarded by
living trees and the flashes of
fire seemed bursts of hope, and if
he just concentrated on these
soaring uprisings of light he
might find asylum, he might even
rise from defense to dogma to some
great edifice of religious light—
"Keep it going," he said, and the crackling,
growing glow illuminated his
search through the surrounding
underbrush for more of anything that
would keep it going.

He understood

He understood that he had no
right, that he had been lucky, that
no war, no serious disaster, no
devastating storm had ever assailed
him, that he had a tight roof over his
head, and ample food and decent
clothes and family and friends and a
delightful wife whose gardening gave
him the embrace of peonies, roses,
rhododendrons, daisies, and so
many other natural benefactions, and
he had a good enough education to
grasp the meaning of *il faut
cultiver notre jardin*, so he had no
right to do otherwise, no right to
go look over the edge of his
blessings, no right to peer outside the
puffy bright cloud he lived
within, no right to crack his
invisible cocoon.

He had merely

He had merely been out exploring when
he fell into a black hole, which became
a concern to all around because they
hadn't known it was there, and considered
being in one an aberration, an alterable
rather than permanent condition, so they
began to think up methods he could
possibly use to get out, which they
decided might be contained in a number
of books that they tossed down to him, and
also they recommended improvements in
the circumstances of his overall life, which
they hollered to him down the hole, and
also, they lowered down some pills that
would give him uplift power, while they
also constructed a set of steps he could
take to get back to level ground, but he
kept trying to tell them, sometimes yelling
it up to the top, that falling into a black
hole was not the problem; the problem was
that black holes exist, that allowable
reality includes places into which one can
fall, that he fell into it because it was
there.

They wanted us

They wanted us to think of him as
just a cat, and cats die, but cats
don't have to be hit by cars to
die, they don't have to come,
gagging on blood from internal
hemorrhaging, out of the
street across the driveway up
the steps to the door into the
house to die, which is to
say they don't have to
come home to die, making
it safely home where a loved
pet shouldn't have to die in
spasms of choking on blood, in
convulsions of gasping for
breath, because lying at
home, even a cat can feel that
breath should come back, but
nothing comes, only unquenchable
blood, which does not stop until
he lies on the floor, the choking finally
over, the convulsive spasms of
his body finally done, and no
pulse, and only a few involuntary
heaves ending the life of a cat
who came home thinking that
if only he could get home, he would
not die, he would be saved, he
would be able to depend
on us.

He hated when

(for Bob Sanders, 1938-2012)

He hated when the
phone rang, hated to pick it
up, hated to say "hello," hated
to feel so relieved when the
caller wanted only to ask him to
vote for somebody or buy
something, would vote for
anybody, buy anything, if
only no one would call and
tell him that still another
person he had cared about all
his long life had—no, had no
preparation for the suddenness
of that, not after all these
years, all these seeming
certainties, all this lifetime of
insulation, all this
busyness, all these
obfuscations that
mankind had been able to
invent over the years, the
centuries, the eons going
back to the caves and the
first chalky visions of
spirits in the swirls of the
campfire smoke, rising now
from cathedral candles, no
he had no preparation for the
dissipation of that smoke, no
way to withstand the increasing
rage and fear he felt whenever he
heard the phone.

He began

(For Richard Hedrich, 1929-2012)

He began out on the porch, sitting,
dedicating a farewell drink to his
friend, and then another, until he
thought that if he drank enough his
friend would reappear, would sit
with him again, as they used to
do in so many evenings and
afternoons, and he knew the
reappearing friend might be an
illusion, but he didn't care, let
it be an illusion, let him
have any illusion he could, any
salving illusion, because what
the hell is anyone without
illusions, and all he asked was
just this one, that his friend could
be back, that the two of
them could have a pleasant
drink together as they had done
so many times through all those
years when they had the
unspoken but wonderful
illusion that they
always could.

That evening

That evening a selected few of
us entered the chambers to
which the Company had given
us invitations—the four square
rooms that together formed a
larger square, the walls and
floors and ceilings all richly
paneled with gleaming
mahogany, where we each
received a cigar such as
one gets to smoke only
once in a lifetime, or
never, tobacco so rare, so
expensive, all rolled into a
shape so perfect, so
exquisite, and we milled in
the rooms and smoked and
talked of how extraordinary
this experience was, watching
the glowing ash hold its
shape and grow at the ends of
our splendid cigars as
delicate wisps of delicious-
smelling smoke slowly curled
around us in the fine rooms, and
when at last only stubs
remained, we took our
leave, thanking the
Company, repeating over and
over how fortunate, how
privileged, we had been, we,
the select few.

Thunder over

Thunder over the sea and leaping
waves lashing the rocks and
sand slipping in, under, and
out, and trees breaking, making
spaces for new shoots to fill the
void, and the void surrounding
and entering all; and out on the
ledge he stumbled and the torrents
roared and the greening void-filling
grass sucked up the rain, and
he clung to roots and knew that
all the acts of cruelty and the
acts of love alike were attempts to
fill the void, and the plants kept
acting in sheer survival to fill it and
even to cover the rocks and smother the
sea with green reaching, reaching
into the void that he could not even
comprehend, the overwhelming
indefinable void that nothing could
ever fill, but he knew that
nonetheless he had to try, he like
everyone and everything else, try
to fill it.

You must perfect

You must perfect your
metaphors they told him, as
if grasping could be
perfected, as if stumbling in
the dark could be
polished, as if groping for a
grip could be purified, as if
staying on one's feet could
be standing up, as if trudging
could be elevated hop-
scotch, as if
asphyxiation could be
manicured, or paradox
painted, or longing
laminated, or, when you
got to the point beyond
which you could see
nothing, you could call it a
remarkable view.

She heard them out

She heard them out in the current, she
watched as they looked for, looked
everywhere, the water moved and
she wished they would quit looking but
she didn't want them to see her because
it was so peaceful, just to be peaceful, just
to watch, and they almost found her, why
did they come to this place, listen and
she would tell them if they wanted to, but
they just wanted to tell, so why didn't
they just, as the water, the water moved on
and came back, moved on and came
back like she could speculate but
she had no reason to tell, no reason to
do anything but watch and see how it
rocked and rocked, back and
forth, time to wait, but why don't you
wait, stay away, stay still, leave
her—"Well, I don't know where she's
gotten to"—shhh, shhh, blue was so rich
flecked with white where they came
together, came back at each other, and
why did they have to get active, get
going, get moving, get up and get
around and get to doing something—"What
in the world are you doing up
here?"—what in the world she was
watching, she watched and now she
couldn't, for the first time in her however
many years of life she screamed as they
picked her up and carried her,
and carried her!

PART EIGHT

Absurd, they said

Absurd, they said, because only
romantic castaway stories have
messages in stoppered bottles surf-
bobbing on edges of mainland
beaches, so they scoffed as they
retrieved, pulled stopper, unfolded
message, and read—w*hat causes the
feeling may be an illusion but*—and
they thought how irritating, how
exasperating, starting with the
improbability of a bottle's
surviving devastating waves, sharp
shore-rocks, myopic sharks, then the
improbability of its containing a
message—dry—inside, or at
least a half-message, as if the fairy
tale could go only so far, leaving
them to imagine the rest of what might
have been written by some Copacabana
drunk who had emptied the bottle, or
a bored stern man playing a trick as the
lobster boat headed in, or a kid in some
summer cottage acting out tales of
Poe, also improbable that one of these
could have concocted such a saying, or
half-saying, so maybe it came from a
Sappho fragmenting on her island, or
a victim of Crusoe's cannibals who
couldn't get the message finished in
time, or a boating Wittgenstein who
didn't want to waste the great line he
couldn't figure how to finish, hoping
somebody else would find and finish
it—all of this assuming, of course, that
the message wasn't finished, that it could
be finished, and that—most improbable of
all—it would make sense if it were.

One child

One child appeared one
night outside his window, looking
in, a question in the child's eyes, and
then two, three, all looking, then
eventually a dozen looking the
question at him, and eventually
hundreds, thousands, until all the
children in the world appeared to
have gathered where he lived, and
stood looking through every
window and crack in his ramshackle
hut, their eyes asking again, and he
knew that he could not deny, he
could not just hammer patches over
the holes and say, see, that's all you
need, because they would pull off the
patches, break through the boards, enter
his house, and insist, and then he would
have to have something real to tell them,
    something they could swing upon,
    laugh and jump and sing upon,
because whatever he might have said to
grownups, clotted and curdled as they
were and wrapped in impenetrable
realms of thick concrete, he could not
just say to children, to all the beg-eyed
children in the world, that he could not
help, that he had nothing to tell even
himself, that he had no idea what
to tell them.

And he remembered

And he remembered a vole running up
the street as he drove by in his
car, tiny burl of gray fur on black
legs so short that skittering appeared
the limit of its hope, so why had it
crept out on open concrete, totally
exposed, and stutter-stepped straight
up the street regardless of risk, even
as the potentially crushing car
slowed, he, the driver feeling an
impulse to cheer as this lump of
lint kept going, apparently terrified not
of a grabbing cat or a smashing
car, but of failing to get some certain
place, and he in the car could have
stopped, chased the skitterer into the
safe ditch, but why do that?!—why
not follow it where it so desperately
wished to go?!—and then the vole did
veer up a side road and disappeared into
underbrush—disappeared maybe into
the place it sought—and he suddenly
found himself longing for that
place, longed for a destination so
significant that killers passing by would
slow, would cheer in hope that he
could get there.

And the snow

And the snow flitted down in all its
seducing beauty, mantling the land-
scape in irreproachable white, so that
    life and I made love again
    upon this glorious morning
    where every harshness disappeared
    beneath sweet flakes descending,
    tiny flakes, gentle flakes,
    how could they hold such sway
    over the thuggish ugliness
    of the ordinary day,
and they kept coming, drifting over the
icy streams, the freezing grasses, the
bare trees, and every sign of human
harm, until all lay in a sheen of
peace so brilliant that it did not
matter whether they all too soon would
melt, run off, leave the world a contentious
mess again—no, he would not believe that
the best could best the worst, but he
could believe that he didn't want to
go yet, didn't want to fade into
oblivion, didn't want to sit some-
where in the snow, let it slowly take
him over too, so easy to go that way, so
easy to let the numbing come, and why
not let it, enjoy its coming in the
splendid snow, before the inevitable
thaw could take the desire to persist
away.

What was less

What was less real about them than
anything else, the little people in the tiny
train station, conversing in the colorful
lit-up shops, sledding down through
the cotton-ball snow, skating on the
mirror of a pond while now and
again the red lights shone and the
crossing-guardrails clanged and the
train—the whistling, chugging
steam-emitting engine with its
cars of all colors and kinds—came
down from the painted hills and
burst into the bright station, and
stopped to take on—but what was
any less real about those people, no
matter that they never got off or
on, no matter that they felt no
need to arrive or depart, no
matter that they were
painted happy no matter
what, and never mind that the
train took off again to go around
and come back and stop and
go around again, and never mind how
happy it all made the junior
engineer who never wanted to turn
the set off for the night and go to bed as
his parents insisted for his own
good that he should and tried to persuade
him that all the little people in the
train station would be all right because
none of them was real.

How he loved

How he loved theology, most
creative of all arts, the one
that filled the skies with
visions of the divine, bright-
eyed and fast fleeting, or steely
eyed and white bearded, giants
with smiling eyes, or odd
gods that assumed all manner of
shimmering shifting shapes, their
outlines radiating from the stars, or
their silhouettes, chariot-carried, in
the rising sun, or perfected
specimens of ourselves, some
thundering and wild, some
loving and milky mild, some
laying down laws gold-scripted on
indestructible slates, but others
misbehaving on the grandest
scale, some demanding worship and
glorification and prayer, some
requiring sacrifice in blood, some
abhorring violence and preaching
peace, some just floating over in
grand indifference, and some peeping
at us out of trees and flowers and
stones as if to see what else, if
properly propitiated, we might decide
could save us.

The waters flowed

The waters flowed in and
out with the tide and
he thought it ought to mean
something, that's what his mind
thought, and then his mind did
metaphysics and saw divinity
swimming in the tide, and then his
mind did mathematics and
saw equations in the ins and
outs, the nows and agains, but
his mind wished to see beyond
its fabrications of order, see
past the barrier of reductive
desire, see beyond the
comfort of resolution, see
past even what his tide-borne
self longed to hear—the
answerless wildness of the
final reply.

Or was he merely

Or was he merely the self-
solicitous field mouse who
assiduously gnawed on a single
kernel discovered amid the
harvested stalks while his
better brothers reveled in the
granary; the mouse without
enough imagination to
inhabit golden piles of
possibility, or see in the
sun's priapic reappearance the
promise of recurrent fruit; the
mouse who read messages in
broken stalks and cold
clods in frost-wracked
fields; the mouse who went
on gnawing into December's
dark, making a mountain out
of an empty corn hill?

Suddenly

Suddenly the words whirled
up and ferociously formed a
circular core, a great vertical
whorl, from whose edges whole
phrases erupted, sought to
emerge, flared, then fell
back to go round and slowly
round, thousands of words or
more, yet none intelligible to
the following eye, if only
one knew what meaning they
made, berserk dictionaries,
diction drunk, syntax spinning,
spitting, stammering back until
all again became fettered and
utterable—
    and they were poems then
    and sparkling fair
    exhausted lay upon the pages
    and stayed there
    slept like nested swallows
    with severed wings
    inertial and determinable
    things.

Goodbye now

Goodbye now, she cannot
say exactly, she cannot be the
time, she waits by the tree, waits
looking upward, she waits for the
word, waits for the moment when she
cares, what she cares for, so
high, so high she cannot tell who they
are, she does not know, cares for so
high up in the air, where, where, tree
tresses in the morning,
    "I know not what, I know not where,
    up in the tree in the morning,
    nor know what is in the sky up there
    come down again in the evening,"
and so she waits to see where they will
take her because she thinks it will be
somewhere because there will be
something to drink but where does she
want, but they too want to go and
quickly go, quickly, and they shift and
she does not, but she cares, but she
does that, and they pick her, pick her
up in the tree and she hears herself
singing,
    "I know not to, I fro not so,
    wait until can it be morning,
    it cannot be, wait just a bit,
    and see if can it be evening,"
and so she sits, waits, waits, sits, she
knows how it cannot last, it cannot
wait until—and then, sleep, come heavily
down, crashing coming down.